My Journey Through Grief and Healing

A Personal Story of Love, Loss, and Finding Peace After Grief

By
S. J. McGuire

Copyright

About The Author

S. J. McGuire is a retired executive and writer living on Long Island, New York, where she shares her home with her beloved pups. After the loss of her husband, she began writing as a way to process her grief and connect with others walking a similar path. *My Journey Through Grief and Healing* is her first book.

Dedication

In loving memory of

WILLIAM PATRICK MCGUIRE

November 10, 2023

Loving husband and dad

Acknowledgement

I wish to express my deepest gratitude to my lovely daughters, Julie and Jessica, whose love, patience, and encouragement carried me through the most difficult days. To my family and friends who have supported me in countless ways, I am forever grateful. A heartfelt thank you to the facilitators and members of the Bereavement Groups I attended; you gave me a safe place to share my sorrow, find understanding, and discover hope again. I also want to acknowledge my beloved pups, Maddie and Ellie, and my sweet grand-pups, Ripley and Marley, whose unconditional love, playful energy, and constant companionship gave me comfort and strength when I needed it most, bringing light to even my darkest days. They reminded me daily of the joy that still exists in life. Finally, I want to thank every reader who opens this book. May my words bring you comfort, encouragement, and the reminder that none of us is ever truly alone on this journey.

Table of Contents

"Even though I walk through the valley of the

shadow of death, I will fear no evil, for

You are with me; Your rod and Your staff,

they comfort me."

--Psalm 23:4

Introduction

I remember sitting in the funeral home on a bright November day staring at the front of the room where my husband, Bill, was laid out. I was filled with an immense sense of grief, but at the same time with a feeling of disbelief. This couldn't be happening… it had to be a terrible nightmare.

Everyone experiences grief at some point in their lives, unfortunately. It is a sad part of life, although if you believe in God, you know that one day we will be reunited with our loved ones, and then for all eternity there will only be joy and peace. Until then, there is reality and daily life to experience and get through.

Grief is an intricate and often overwhelming emotion that can take many forms. The relationship of the deceased will affect the depth of the grief as well. I know grief is grief, but it is different each time. When we read or see on the news the devastation, tragedies, and deaths that occur daily in our world, we grieve. However, it usually does not tear a hole in our hearts. We offer prayers and mourn them, but soon you put the incident behind you. When it is a parent, spouse, child, close relative, or close friend, the pain cuts deep into our hearts. We are unable to be unaffected by the loss.

When I lost my father and 14 years later my mother, it was devastating. I mourned deeply, of course. My parents had lived with us in a two-family house, so we were together every day. I was in my early 50s when my mom passed, and she helped raise our daughters while Bill and I both worked. While we grieved, we were kept busy and distracted with the day-to-day activities of everyday life.

Life moves on, and your children go off on their own. You believe you have all this time with your spouse. You make plans, focus more on each other as you are retired now. Then COVID hit, and we were isolated for almost a year. We downsized and moved to a much smaller house. We settled in, made some renovations, and were looking forward to taking some more trips together. Within less than two months of being diagnosed, my husband, Bill, was gone before any treatment could begin.

By telling about my journey, a journey that never truly ends… just changes, I thought that some of my experiences could help others going through similar grief. I am not a professional therapist, nor do I offer an outline of the "grieving process" as I believe this will differ from person to person. These are just my experiences that may help others to be able to reach out and move on, one day at a time.

"Though He brings grief, He will show compassion so great is His unfailing love."

--Lamentations 3:32

CHAPTER ONE

Leaving

"CODE BLUE, CODE BLUE" was heard reverberating around Bill's room and the hospital corridor. I was ushered out of his room while the hospital team worked on him. I remember sitting in the hallway, sobbing. My daughter, Julie, was trying to find out what was going on. One moment I was sitting next to him in his hospital room (eating the strawberry ice cream he didn't want that was melting), and the next moment I was observing him getting very agitated. He was supposed to start some radiation treatment after dinner, but the nurse said she was going to recommend it be postponed as he seemed weak. Then he suddenly sat upright, staring straight ahead, and yelled out the name "Lenny." I said Who is Lenny? He said annoyingly, "Lenny Carroll," like he saw him, but the name was not familiar to me from the people he had known since sharing his life with me. His nurse saw this transpire and started asking for team assistance while I was led out of his room.

The following hours and days were a blur… a nightmare, really, that is forever etched in my memory. Bill had suffered a major cardiac arrest resulting from his organs shutting down due to his advanced illness. They put him on life support, allowing my other daughter,

Jessica, who was on a plane on her way to New York City, to get to see her dad and for us and his brother to be able to say our final goodbyes. A priest was called in again, which was very important to Bill, and he also spent time with us as Bill was eventually detached from the machines that were keeping his heart beating. His presence during this time was spiritually helpful. Making the arrangements, the funeral, greeting family and visitors is still a blur… I was numb.

I'm sure all your stories are similar in one way or another. All the "what ifs" that go through your head, why hadn't his doctors seen that something was wrong? One way to look at it is that his downhill health happened so quickly, he didn't suffer for long, and he went peacefully. Truthfully, Bill would not have handled the treatment that was ahead of him very well, so he was spared much pain and worry. However, whether it is a long illness or happens suddenly, the result is the same… You are alone! Your other half, with whom you spent so many years together, is gone. The person who knew me so well was no longer here, whether to hug or annoy me. It's funny, but the things that annoyed me most about Bill at times were also the things I would miss most. In my case, we had been together for a total of 55 years. We were married for fifty-one years and seven months and were very fortunate to have gotten to celebrate our 50th wedding anniversary with family and friends. I feel blessed and thankful for having had this time together. However, whatever time you have with a loved one is never long enough.

While Bill was at the first hospital, going through tests, and doctors kept telling me that "he is a very sick man," I kept thinking, "I don't want to be alone." My daughters kept saying, "You are not alone, Mom". The truth is, I was. They had their own lives and were deeply grieving themselves. The first year since his passing was especially difficult for all of us. I didn't want to drag them down further, so I did my best to do my grieving when I was alone. While in my car running errands or when I was alone in the house, I would let the tears flow. I would ask again and again, "Why did you leave me?"

Our dog Maddie, a cava doodle, is my angel and gave me so much solace. I don't know what I would have done without her. She comforts me still. On days when I would have loved to put the covers over my head and stay in bed, I knew I couldn't. Maddie needed me. Bill loved Maddie so much, too. Maddie is such an affectionate dog and is always by my side, and is my constant companion.

We were fortunate to be able to get a golden doodle for Jessica shortly after Bill passed, which she named Ellie. I didn't want her to feel so alone when she went back to Florida. Bill spent a lot of time with her there in our condo, and I knew it would be lonely for her. Ellie and Maddie love to play and are so funny together. They are so sweet and make me laugh with their escapades. I also watch Julie's dogs occasionally, so it can be a busy household at times. Since I do not have any grandchildren, my dog and my grand pups help keep me upbeat and active, and do not judge if I am feeling melancholy.

They seem to understand and cuddle closer. I realize that having dogs may not be for everyone. They do limit your ability to travel and other activities. In my case, they have been my lifeline in my journey. Each of you must find what works best for you.

"Do not be discouraged, for the Lord

Your God will be with you

wherever you go."

--Joshua 1:9

CHAPTER TWO

Life Alone

You can feel alone even when in a crowd. You can't understand that until you have lost your other half. Bill passed about two weeks before Thanksgiving in 2023. Normally, that was the holiday I would prepare for family and friends. I dreaded the upcoming holidays. Bill's passing was too fresh. My niece held Thanksgiving that year. I was there with my daughter, Jessica, but might as well have been alone as I didn't feel part of the gathering. I was still numb. Then there would be Christmas to get through.

Jess went back to the condo in Florida till almost Christmas as she was still working remotely. Her apartment in Manhattan was rented. Julie lives in Manhattan and teaches in the Bronx. She spends her weekends upstate at our house, being very much a nature girl. Skiing, skinning, and hiking would be her outlet and help her through the grieving process. We had our house upstate since the girls were very young, so there were many memories there.

My daughters didn't want me to just ignore the holidays, so I decorated a little for Christmas to please them. My heart wasn't in it, and I remember crying while decorating. I talked to Bill a lot.

Sometimes, I would be angry at him and would always ask, "Why did you leave me?" This was a refrain I would often say in the weeks and months that followed.

Everyone says the first year after losing a loved one is the most difficult… so many "firsts." First holidays, birthdays, anniversaries, and even mundane things like the first time going to the supermarket, especially when Bill would be the one to go most times. First time making dinner, seeing friends, getting in the car and driving, doing laundry (Bill especially liked to do the laundry all the time), and anything that you did before when he was here, becomes a first for you doing it alone. Fortunately, I was the one who handled the bills and our finances, so that was not an issue. However, he took care of the maintenance of our cars, registration renewals, inspections, heavy lifting around the house, and having heating systems and air-conditioning maintained or arranged for service at our properties. Although I would do all the Christmas decorating myself, mainly because I'm a perfectionist and drive everyone crazy, Bill would take it all down for me. Then I would pack up everything so it was organized for the following year.

I had to change ownership on vehicles and figure out how to handle the vehicle in his name in Florida… the list goes on and on, as I am sure everyone can relate. Fortunately, while I faced these various challenges, my working career experience in implementing changes and solving problems for a growing company helped me considerably to navigate situations I had not been familiar with.

I have found that for me, everything is just… different. Some people like to say it becomes a new "normal." Regardless, it is a learning curve that I did not want to partake. A club I did not want to be part of. My loss forever altered the fabric of my existence. In time, you realize that you are more resilient than you thought, and somehow you will face your loss. Even though the path ahead is uncertain, you realize that as you face each challenge, you are capable and have the strength to do the things you relied on your loved one for in the past. Some of that will bolster your confidence, and you may feel a renewed sense of purpose and strength to embrace the challenges ahead.

So, what do you do when faced with these circumstances? What can you do to try to understand and grapple with the array of emotions you feel constantly? I did seek out Bereavement Groups. I felt that being with people who are feeling and going through the same emotions as me had to be helpful. A family member involved in pastoral activities on Long Island gave me a list of Catholic churches that offer Bereavement Group meetings during the year. I called them and was notified when they would have a group starting, and I could sign up. Otherwise, I would know only of the groups my parish offered since each parish advertised solely in their church's weekly bulletin. There was no central location that listed these meetings. As a result, I ended up participating in four different Bereavement Groups. Each Bereavement Group was different because of the dynamics of various individuals attending and the facilitators' experience. I gained insight and help from each group and made friends. Some of us continue to meet in either "moving on groups," lunches or dinners, or other social groups. We understand how we each feel, so there is no need to explain anything and no judgment. It is so heartwarming to be with people who "get you" and be able to laugh again and share stories.

At the Bereavement meetings, the participants would discuss some of the problems they were facing and their emotions. It was very interactive, and participants would share their own experiences as well as offer suggestions. We were all experiencing the same emotions, so it was very helpful to hear how others were handling certain challenges. I have had some people say to me, "But isn't it depressing being with people who are also sad?" Truthfully, only people who have experienced a loss like you have can truly understand what you are going through. Others will say, "It has been long enough," "Time to move on," "Start going out again," etc. They are not in your shoes and until they are, they cannot understand the depth of your emotions, regardless of how well-meaning they may be.

He will wipe away every tear from their

eyes, and death shall be no more, neither

shall there be mourning, nor crying,

nor pain anymore, for the former things have
passed away."

--Revelations 21:4

CHAPTER THREE

Dealing with Your Emotions

What do you do when you are in a public place or family event and the tears just come? This has happened to me many times. While I try to grieve in private so as not to make anyone uncomfortable, there are times you can't help it. I remember shedding tears at one of my great nieces' christenings. Bill had been with me at the previous one. It was less than a year since Bill had passed, and I couldn't help the tears that were flowing while sitting in church, so I left the church and stood outside, hoping the fresh air would help calm me. It was a difficult afternoon. I just felt especially alone even in the crowd that day, and at the table, unintentionally, there was an empty seat next to me that didn't help the situation. During most of the first year and even later, I found myself avoiding large gatherings because they would make me feel more alone. Eventually, it gets a little bit better, but each person will be different.

Often in church at Mass, I feel the tears well up in my eyes. Bill would always get annoyed at me because I would always be late for Mass. I hear him in my head saying, "I see you slipping in late." Sometimes it could be that the homily just strikes a chord with you. It can be seeing a contemporary couple together that makes me wistful and wishing Bill was with me. Whenever your emotions affect you, do not feel you need to apologize for it. It is natural to feel this way, and it does get somewhat better with time.

It is important that you do grieve, however. Sometimes you may think that if you just keep yourself busy, you will be able to deal with this loss. When my mother went to be with our Lord in 1999, we had just moved into a new, large house that had been built for us. When she passed a couple of months later, I was so busy with my career, decorating the new house, landscaping, and my family, I did not give myself enough time to grieve, preferring to stay busy. However, six months later, it caught up with me. I began to have a lot of anxiety and went to a therapist. I just started crying as soon as I walked into her office. You may want to act strong after suffering a loss, but it is very important to grieve. The delayed reaction was like having PTSD (post-traumatic stress disorder). It will catch up with you if not dealt with.

Some may feel that doing something in their loved ones' memory brings comfort. Honoring Bill's memory became a crucial part of my healing journey. I found a great deal of comfort in making keepsakes. Since Bill passed just before Thanksgiving and Christmas holidays, making things in his memory brought solace and helped occupy my time. I ordered a bracelet for my daughter that had a magnifying viewer with a picture of Bill in it. I then ordered a gold heart locket for my other daughter as a Christmas gift. I created ornaments for our different Christmas trees with his picture.

Besides personalized gifts, I created a photo book celebrating Bill's life and ordered three of them, one for each of my daughters and myself. Each activity helped me feel that Bill was by my side and close to me. When spring finally arrived, I made a little meditation corner on my deck in the backyard with a fountain and plants, and a chime that was also dedicated to Bill. I love to sit in the rocking chair in the meditation corner and think of all our memories together. Sometimes, I pray or read or just have some quiet time with my dogs by my side. Whenever the wind would make the chimes ring, I felt Bill was near and visiting, which I would find very comforting.

There will always be moments of sadness regardless of what you do. It is totally normal to feel that sadness. Sometimes I hug Bill's clothes that are still hanging in his closet if I just feel I need to feel him close. I plan to have quilts made from his clothing for each of us to wrap around us and feel like Bill is giving us a big hug. So far, I have a stuffed Teddy bear and rabbit made of his clothing for each of my daughters, which they received as gifts this past Christmas, along with the Shutterfly photo books celebrating Bill's life. I am also in the process of having a quilted pattern made using his colorful ties that I will have framed and hang as artwork. I had done something similar with pieces of my mother's clothing. Whenever I walk by the framed pattern I have hanging in my kitchen, each piece of her clothing brings back memories.

After finding comfort in creating my own keepsakes, I began looking into other online options that might help others as well. If you are crafty and like to make items yourself, that's great! However, there are many online organizations that you can order memorial gifts from, such as Shutterfly, Etsy, Bradford Exchange, and various jewelry companies. You can have mugs, blankets, or pillows with photos or special sayings made, too. You can just Google: memorial jewelry, quilts, bears, and any item you can think of. A list of many different companies will appear. These items make great gifts for family members or close friends, and some mementoes for yourself. I am not recommending you turn your house into a shrine, just some touches that bring comfort.

I did find that sometimes, a few new items in the house to refresh things can be calming. It can be as simple as a new comforter, area rug, or new towels. You are not erasing the person, but sometimes little changes are helpful. Perhaps there is something your loved one had wanted to have done or some renovation that you can proceed with. Then again, some may feel the need to move to something smaller, with less maintenance. Whatever works for you is what you should do, but I caution you to try not to make any major decisions in the first year, as you may not be thinking clearly yet.

I have also ordered a memorial brick at my parish church in Our Lady of Lourdes grotto garden, which I can visit at any time when I can't make the trip to the cemetery where he is interred. I often like taking walks with Ellie and Maddie to the garden and saying a little prayer by those bricks.

If you have a charity or grant you wish to establish with an organization in your loved one's name, that is another way to honor them.

At some point, I plan to take a trip to Medjugorje in Bosnia, where the visionaries still periodically see our Blessed Mother. Bill had heard me say many times that I wanted to visit there. When he was sick, he said he wanted to go with me after his treatment. I plan to make that journey in his memory since we never got the chance to do it together.

"God helps those who help

Themselves"

--Algernon Sidney, Theorist

CHAPTER FOUR

Helping Yourself

The foregoing has been about what you can do to keep your loved one close and honor them. Now you must think about yourself. You may not want to, but you must! Maybe like me, you like to garden, take up a new hobby, or get back to one you used to like to do. You may have a talent you can share or perhaps volunteer and help others. Perhaps you can take cooking lessons either out of necessity or for fun, or learn to sketch or paint, or go to the gym and work out. Even just walking in a park or in your neighborhood can be enjoyable, especially if you find a walking partner. It could be that you always wanted to learn to play an instrument or learn a language. There are so many apps out there to help you do almost anything. Most of these involve interacting with others and will help you get out of your shell.

I decided to brush up on my Italian since I had not spoken it since before my mother passed. I downloaded one of the many language apps available and practiced speaking again. I also have always wanted to learn to play the piano. Since I have the piano that my daughters took their early lessons on years ago, I can teach myself by watching YouTube. I have a list of things I would like to do besides my normal "To-Do" list. Both will keep me energized and from getting bored. Making such lists can keep you motivated and active.

I personally also love to read, watch television shows and movies, garden, and play with my dogs, but I know it is necessary to interact more. It would be easy for me to become a hermit since I do appreciate alone time. However, I try to be more social. I enjoy being with both my friends of many years, as well as those I have met on my journey. It may feel difficult at first, but one small step at a time, and you will realize you are able to laugh again.

 It is comforting to remember the wonderful memories and to laugh. Moments of tears may happen less as time goes on. It does not mean you have moved on, but you understand that your loved one would want you to continue living your life until one day you are together. What a joyous day that will be, but you don't want to rush it either. There are still things you are meant to do. It is why you are still here. This is your chance to reinvent yourself and spread your wings, and maybe have a "Second Act" in your life, even though it may be difficult to imagine doing so early on.

You may find yourself with another special friendship or relationship. Your loved one would not want you to be alone, so if you are lucky enough to be able to share your life with someone special, try to remember that your loved one may have arranged to bring that person into your life.

A message from our loved ones:

"Though I may seem far away

We will never truly part,

For part of me lives on FOREVER

There within your Heart.

May Heaven's Light shine on you,

And Remember now and then,

I am with You Always

Until we meet Again."

Do you not know that your bodies are temples

Of the Holy Spirit, who is in you, whom you have

received from God? You are not your own; you

were bought at a price. Therefore, honor God

with your bodies.

--Corinthians 6:19-20

CHAPTER FIVE

Be Mindful of Your Health

Losing a loved one is one of life's most painful experiences, and amid the grief, it can feel almost impossible to focus on your own well-being. Yet caring for your health during this time is essential. Grief places a tremendous strain not only on the heart and mind, but also on the body—disrupting sleep, appetite, and energy.

My health was something I always took for granted. Even though Bill did not have a long illness, unlike many others, where your health becomes secondary to your partner's battle, I still neglected it. With the loss and life adjustments after Bill passed, seeing doctors for my well-being was far from my mind.

I have always been someone who craved sweets, carbs, and dairy… not a very healthy combination long term. I ate what I wanted when I wanted. Cooking was not enjoyable for just myself, so I would take out and whatever was simple. Inevitably, that included sweets that were playing havoc with my body. It took a physical exam I finally got around to, to show me how far I had strayed from a healthy diet. My poor eating habits were not sustainable for the long term. If I wanted to have the longevity that my brothers, parents, and grandparents enjoyed, I needed to make drastic changes. It was a warning and very definitely the wakeup call I needed!

If it weren't for my daughter, Jessie—her perseverance, sacrifices, and unwavering belief that I must do better—I might never have made the changes that turned my health around and quite possibly saved my life. I regret that I often took her help, and even her well-meaning nagging, for granted. At times, I found it irritating, yet she never gave up on me. She guided me toward the right doctors and kept me on course. Jessie has her father's determination; once she knows she's right, she doesn't back down. She was deeply worried about me, and I will always be eternally grateful for her love and persistence.

It is hard to admit, but I had been selfish. Not intentionally, but the result was the same. I was thinking only of myself and was not aware of the effect it would have on my daughters. They were truly afraid that something would happen to me. They had lost one parent less than two years before and didn't want to lose me, too. In addition, there were many things that I still wanted to do and accomplish for myself. It is so easy to fall into a pattern of self-neglect when your world is turned upside down. Yes, we can be sad, we can mourn, but we need to be aware of our loved ones and how our poor choices will affect them.

My advice is that no matter how deep your sadness is, your health is something you need to be very mindful of. It is not selfish to think about your health when grieving… it is a way of honoring both yourself and the one you have lost. By supporting your body, you create more resilience to face the long and often unpredictable waves of emotion. Tending to our health gives us the best chance of finding light again after the darkness.

"Blessed are those who mourn,

For they shall be comforted."

--Matthew 5:4

CHAPTER SIX

Signs

One of the things we spoke about a great deal in the Bereavement Groups I attended is signs from our loved ones. We were all hurting so much that we wanted to feel they were near and that they were alright. Indeed, our loved ones do send us signs. Some may be more obvious than others.

My husband passed a few months before our 52nd wedding anniversary. Since my older daughter, Julie, was going to be on spring break, I suggested we go on a road trip with the dogs to Vermont, as her birthday was a couple of days before our wedding anniversary. She thought it was a great idea, and so we packed up and went. We stopped at our house in the Catskills and then departed from there the next morning. We rented a condo near Stowe, VT, for a few days. The night before our anniversary, I was walking the pups outside. It was deserted in the back as ski season was over and most of the condos were empty. There were a lot of pine needles and branches on the ground. I was feeling very melancholy as it was another "first" holiday without Bill, and his birthday would be in a couple of weeks also. I was looking at the ground and saw a folded $10 bill being held down by a small pine branch. You must admit that it was something strange to find on a cold spring evening with no one around. Bill had passed on the tenth of November, so the $10 "bill" was meaningful. I was sure he was sending me a message that he was with me, and it brought tears to my eyes.

Then I remembered a few days earlier, I had been in a supermarket. I was in one of the aisles on the opposite end of the checkout area, and I was the only person in the aisle. I happened to look down and found a folded $10 bill. I didn't think it was real at first. Having worked in Manhattan my entire career, I was used to seeing what looked like paper money only to pick it up and realize there was an advertisement on the other side. This was real money, and then, with what happened a few days later in Vermont, I was sure Bill was sending me a message that he was remembering our anniversary, and he was near.

A woman in one of the groups I attended had told us that she had gone to a casino on her 80th birthday and won $5,000! She felt it was a gift from her husband. I guess Bill may have seemed not as generous in comparison, but it is the thought that counts, and I was so grateful for that sign.

There is such a feeling of wanting to know our loved one is all right. You may feel that person beside you at times or smell something that reminds you of them. I remember being at our house upstate and waking up and smelling bacon in the kitchen. Bill loved bacon and felt he was letting me know he was around. No one had cooked bacon or anything else, so I believe that was a message. Maybe they do not have bacon in heaven, and Bill was craving some. Anyway, it made me smile.

I remember the summer my mom passed in 1999. She had planted a peach tree from a pit of a peach she had eaten while we were all upstate. A tree grew, and that September it produced such large, ripe, and juicy peaches. I was not up much that summer, but we had someone trimming trees, and he told us he hoped we didn't mind that he took a couple of peaches. He had never seen such large, juicy peaches. The following spring, the tree was no more. It was a final gift.

I also remember weeding some plant boxes the following spring, and when I got to the last one, it was weeded and there were petunias growing. My mom, who loved to garden, was giving me another gift and saying to me that she was near and would be "forever near." Nowadays, every time I am out planting or in the garden, I turn around and look at the butterflies fluttering around and ask my mom if she likes what I planted. The butterflies flutter as if to nod and then fly away. My heart is filled with joy at that connection.

The need to know about our loved one can be so strong that some of us may feel compelled to visit a psychic/medium that may be able to connect and give us some insight. While it may be unorthodox and something the church frowns upon, if it gives you some comfort, then do so. Just make sure it is someone authentic and may be referred to you, as there are so many that can prey on your situation.

I used to have fun psychic parties at my house where a psychic/medium I know would sit privately with the people at my party, so I am familiar with them. When Bill passed, there was such a feeling of wanting to know he was alright that I visited a couple of psychics on different occasions. Both times, I was told that Bill had trouble crossing over as he did not understand what was happening. He was probably looking down on himself when the medical team disconnected him from the life support machines. I can hear him say, "Wait, wait, what is going on here?" I can see him being very perplexed by that experience. The psychic said that someone was sent to assist him. Another said it was his uncle John with whom he had been close.

They also said that Bill would comment on how great he looks. You are your very best self in heaven… no pain, no wrinkles, no disabilities, and you have your youth back (and Bill probably had his hair back too, as he hated going bald). My mother would always come through when I visited psychics in the past and would comment on how great she looks, too. So don't judge those who visit a psychic/medium, since if it brings peace of mind, then it is worthwhile if you are reasonable and open-minded about the experience. Again, just be very careful that you visit someone who is reputable.

You may have heard about seeing signs from your loved ones, such as cardinals, butterflies, or finding coins on the ground. Some may say they don't believe in these "signs." However, if it brings you comfort, who is there to say it isn't true? It could be flickering lights, a special song you hear on the radio at just the right moment, a scent in the air, a note you find, or a television that suddenly turns on by itself. If it makes you feel your loved one is near, cherish those signs that bring a little joy into your heart. I personally believe in all those signs, and they bring me much peace at times when I need it most.

The Lord is near to the

brokenhearted and saves the crushed

In spirit.

--Psalms 34:18

CHAPTER SEVEN

Faith

Where would we be without our faith in God, the creator? I can't imagine going through life without it. When you have done all that you can about a situation, pray and let go and let God handle it. We may not see a way, but God always has a way and answers in His time, not our timing. This can be frustrating, but understand we are being tested, so it is important to stay true to our faith, no matter how difficult.

Our faith is challenged frequently in life. The losses we suffer may make us angry with God. Why did He let this happen? I have been faithful, so why do I have to suffer like this? We must understand that our faith does not exempt us from suffering, but He does promise that He will help us through it and "bring beauty for our ashes."

How can we find anything positive about our loss? That is a question we often ask ourselves. We are plagued with feelings of helplessness; why, what ifs, regrets, could we have done anything to prevent it? It is the circle of life. This life is not the end… the best is yet to come, where there will be no more pain, suffering, or sadness. However, it is difficult to rationalize your loss and your faith when it happens. It is important to live our time here to the fullest. We are here for a reason and need to find a renewed sense of purpose and a willingness to embrace whatever challenges and opportunities lie ahead. This may take time to understand. There is a feeling of giving up initially. This is where we need our faith to help us find the strength to carry on.

We are taught that Death does not have the final say. Yes, it is the enemy that will be destroyed, and Jesus has crushed death in His resurrection. Hope of the resurrection frees us to enjoy life again. The life-changing valley of grief also increases our appreciation for life. It allows us to have peace and be able to offer comfort as we look forward to the day when we will never need to say goodbye again.

"The Lord gives strength to His

People: the Lord blesses His people

With peace."

--Psalm 29:11

CHAPTER EIGHT

Moving On

With time, I have begun to look toward the future with a sense of hope and possibility. My journey through grief has equipped me with a deeper understanding of myself and a heightened appreciation for the fragility of life. I am determined to move on in a way that will honor both my past and my future aspirations.

As I continue to navigate the ebb and flow of grief, I have come to accept that life will never be the same. I miss Bill and always will, and his loss has forever altered my life. I will continue to honor him and relive our memories through my projects. However, my journey has taught me that even in the face of profound loss, there is always the potential for renewal and transformation. This journey has been a testament to the resilience of the human spirit.

I had experienced loss through the death of my parents and friends. Those losses were devastating, but at those times of my life, I was engrossed in my career, my husband, and raising our daughters. Fortunately, Bill and I did have the opportunity to travel through the years, especially as the girls were on their own. However, there was more that we wanted to do, and now we would not be able to do it together. For over 55 years together as my other half, I was never truly alone. We always had each other.

Grief will always be a part of my story, but it does not define me. I will draw strength from my grief, and it will become a source of deeper connection to the world around me. This journey through grief and healing is ongoing. As I continue to walk this path, I will do so with the knowledge that healing is not forgetting, but finding the courage to live fully and authentically, even in the face of loss.

You are not forgotten, loved one

Nor will you ever be

As long as life and memory last

We will remember thee

We miss you now, our hearts are sore.

As time goes by, we miss you more,

Your loving smile, your gentle face,

No one can take your vacant place.

I would love to hear from you.

If this book has touched you in some way, or if you would like to share your own experiences, please feel free to reach out. Hearing your stories and reflections not only encourages me, but also continues the circle of connection and support that inspired me to write.

You can send your comments and thoughts to me at: sjmcguire25@gmail.com